A TASTE OF CHICKEN SOUP FOR THE TEENAGE SOUL III

More Stories of Life, Love and Learning

Jack Canfield
Mark Victor Hansen
Kimberly Kirberger

Health Communications, Inc.
Deerfield Beach, Florida

www.hcibooks.com
www.chickensoup.com

Experience Is a Teacher. Reprinted by permission of Julia Travis. ©2000 Julia Travis.

Why Rion Should Live. Reprinted by permission of Sarah Barnett. ©2000 Sarah Barnett.

My Best Friend. Reprinted by permission of Lisa Rothbard. ©2000 Lisa Rothbard.

Healing with Love. Reprinted by permission of Cecile Wood. ©2000 Cecile Wood.

Ghost Mother. Reprinted by permission of Michele Bender. ©2000 Michele Bender.

Terri Jackson. Reprinted by permission of Sydney Fox. ©2000 Sydney Fox.

A Name in the Sand. Reprinted by permission of Elizabeth Stumbo. ©2000 Elizabeth Stumbo.

Inner Sustenance. Reprinted by permission of Michelle Wallace Campanelli. ©2000 Michelle Wallace Campanelli.

Center Stage. Reprinted by permission of Jane Denitz Smith. ©2000 Jane Denitz Smith.

Finding a Vision. Reprinted by permission of Talina Sessler-Barker. ©2000 Talina Sessler-Barker.

Library of Congress Cataloging-in-Publication Data is on file with the Library of Congress

ISBN 0-7573-0341-2

Publisher: Health Communications Inc.
3201 SW 15th Street, Deerfield Beach, FL 33442

We dedicate this book to all the teenagers who sent us their courageous stories and their heartfelt thank-yous.

Contents

Introduction

The Faces of Our Youth

Many older people seem to take an unmerited pride in the mere fact they are adults.
When youth comes crashing in on them with enthusiasm and ideals, they put on their most patronizing smiles and send them out with what they call their blessings.
But you and I know that they have not given their blessings but a cold shower.
They pat the young man or young woman on the back and say:
"You're young. Enjoy your enthusiasm and your ideals while you can.
For when you grow up and grow out into the world you'll see how foolish your ideas actually were."
And, the trouble is, young people do grow up and grow away from their ideals.
And that is one reason why the world into which they go gets better so slowly.

Franklin Delano Roosevelt
32nd President of The United States of America

Experience Is a Teacher

The true test of character is not how much we know how to do, but how we behave when we don't know what to do.

John Holt

I was shaking when I heard the car pull into the driveway. I blamed it on the chill in my house, although most likely it was because of my uncontrollable nerves. When I opened the door, Becca was standing on my porch with a smile plastered on her face.

"Hey," she said. As she stepped inside the doorway, the guys behind her became visible. "Oh, ya," she added. "This is Dan, Josh and Kevin."

"Hi," I said, and they replied the same in

unison. They looked kind of like deer in headlights, standing outside the door, hands jammed in pockets, mouths half-open. As Becca made her way into the house, the guys followed her, and I felt awkwardly lost, unsure of what to say. To avoid forced conversation, I took the opportunity to jot a note to my mom, explaining where I was going.

Eventually, we made it out of the house, and I found myself in the back seat of a navy-blue truck, wedged between Josh and Kevin, two older guys from a different school. Becca was chattering away in the passenger seat, changing the radio station and singing along. My legs began to shake, a sure indicator of my nervousness, and I had to put my hands on my thighs to steady them. We soon reached the restaurant, and I was thankful for the chance to get out of the truck.

Dan was toying with the miniature coffee creamers at the end of the table. "I don't trust these," he announced. "They've probably been sitting here since 1982."

At the opposite end of the table, next to Kevin, I giggled, probably for the eighth time since we'd sat down. I wanted to smack myself. Between my legs shaking and my ridiculous giggling, my immature nervous habits were driving me crazy, and I prayed that nobody else noticed.

Suddenly, Becca stood up. "I have to call my mom. Dan, come with me."

"Um, I'll come, too," I said. Feeling the need to elaborate, I continued, "I have to call my mom, too." I felt stupid following Becca and Dan out to the lobby, like a girl in elementary school who can't go anywhere without her best friend.

As we waited while Becca called her mom, Dan nudged me and said, "So, what do you think of Josh and Kevin?"

"Josh is pretty cute," I said, figuring that honesty was the best way to go.

"Not Kevin?" Dan's eyes sparkled, and I knew what Becca had been talking about when she said how wonderful he was.

"No . . ." I looked out the window. "But don't tell him that I said that."

"I won't." Of course he wouldn't. What did I think this was, elementary school? I felt like a child in a world of adults, unsure how to act or what to say.

"Josh thinks you're really hot," Dan continued.

His statement immediately grabbed my attention. "Oh, really?" I was flattered.

Becca hung up the phone and caught the end of our conversation, saying excitedly, "You have to sit by him when we go back to the table!"

"No," I protested. "That'll look dumb."

"No it won't," she insisted, and Dan agreed.

"Yeah, we'll just move stuff around or whatever." It was obvious that this was an argument I was not going to win.

When we returned to the table and assumed our new seats, Josh didn't say anything. I wondered if he had figured out our juvenile plan, and then I wondered if he even cared. But I quickly tried to brush the thoughts out of my head and proceeded to giggle at everything Dan said.

Next we went to the movies. Without Becca next to me in the theater, I felt completely defenseless. I gripped my knees for support, angry at myself for being nervous. Why couldn't I have more self-confidence and be as charming as other girls are? I leaned my head back against the headrest, watching Dan and Becca out of the corner of my eye. No contact yet, I noted. I didn't know what to do with my hands, and it seemed like they took on a life of their own as they repetitiously roamed from my knees to my thighs and eventually gripped the edge of my purse.

I felt a nudge on my right arm. I looked over at Dan and watched as he mouthed the words, "Make a move." He then grinned at me and raised his eyebrows in Josh's direction.

"No!" I whispered emphatically.

"Why not?" he replied with a kind of urgency.

I half-shrugged my shoulders. "I don't know." How could I explain to him the way my mind works? I could never "make a move" on anyone; I didn't have the nerve. My fear of rejection was too intense. Out of the corner of my eye, I saw that Becca was leaning on Dan's shoulder, and his hand was resting on her knee. I sank farther into my seat.

On the way home from the movies, Becca asked Dan if he had a piece of paper. I knew immediately what she was doing and wanted to object, but couldn't. When she handed me Josh's number on a torn piece of paper, I didn't even look at it. I just played with it between my fingers, bending the edges and running it along the folds of my jeans. Josh's reaction to the piece of paper in his hand was similar.

We pulled into my driveway, and I thought that I was finally safe at home as I said good-bye to everyone and sauntered up to my porch. But as I turned around to give a final wave good-bye, I found Josh standing on the lawn.

"Hey," he said, in a way only older guys can. "When are you going to be home tomorrow?"

"Probably all day," I managed and immediately thought of how dumb I sounded.

"Okay, then. I'll, um, call you around one."

I flashed a slight smile. "Okay. Bye!" I stepped inside my house, allowing myself to breathe only when I had closed the door and was safe inside.

I washed my face, wondering if he would think that I was "really hot" without makeup.

As I curled up in bed, the phrase "If only I had . . ." crossed my mind so many times that I became exhausted. But then I remembered that experience, even if awkward and uncomfortable, or in the form of a guy named Josh, is always a teacher. With that, I gradually fell asleep, knowing tomorrow was a new day, and I could rest assured there would be more lessons to learn.

Julia Travis

Why Rion Should Live

Believe that life is worth living and your belief will help create the fact.

WILLIAM JAMES

High school didn't frighten me. Oh sure, the endless halls and hundreds of classrooms were overwhelming, but I took it in with all the pleasure of starting a new adventure. My freshman year was full of possibilities and new people. With a class of nearly two thousand newcomers, you just couldn't go wrong. So I, still possessing the innocence of a child concealed in a touch of mascara and lipstick, set out to meet them all.

Spanish One introduced me to Rion. By the student definition, he was a "freak:" the black jeans, the well-worn Metallica shirts, the wallet chains, the works. But his unique personality and family troubles drew me to him. Not a crush, more of a curiosity. He was fun to talk to, and where interrupted whispering sessions left off, hours of phone conversations picked up.

During one of these evening conversations, "it," as we like to address the incident, unfolded. We were discussing the spectacular height of Ms. Canaple's over-styled bangs when I heard Rion's dad yelling in the background. "Hold on," Rion muttered before a question could be asked. I could tell that he was trying to muffle the receiver, but you could still hear the horror as if his room were a dungeon, maximizing the bellows. Then the line went dead.

Shaking, I listened to the flatline of the phone for a minute before gently placing it in its cradle, too scared to call back for fear of what I might hear. I had grown up in an ideal family setting: a mom and a dad and an older sister as a role model. This kind of situation took me by surprise, and I felt confused and helpless at the same time. A couple of tense hours later, after his father had gone to bed,

Rion called me to apologize. He told me his dad had received a letter from his ex-wife, Rion's mom, saying she refused to pay child support. Having no other scapegoat, he stumbled into Rion's room in rage.

"I can't take this anymore. All the fighting . . . it's always there. . . ." His voice had trailed off, lost in painful thought. "All I have to do is pull the trigger, and it will be over."

"No!" I screamed. "Don't talk like that! You know you have so much to live for." It was becoming clearer every second how threatening the situation was. A cold, forced chuckle came from the other end of the line. "Yeah, right," was his response. We got off the phone, but only after promising to go right to sleep.

Sleep, however, was light years away from me. I was so worried and had a feeling I was Rion's only hope. He had told me repeatedly that it was hard to open up to anyone but me. How could someone not want to live? I could literally list the reasons why I loved waking up every morning. Frantically, I racked my brain for ways to convince Rion of this. Then the lightbulb clicked on. I took a piece of notebook paper and entitled it, "Why Rion Should Live." Below, I began listing every reason I could think of that a person had to exist. What started as a few sentences turned into twenty, then thirty-two, then forty-seven. By midnight, I had penned fifty-seven reasons for Rion to live. The last ten were as follows:

48) Six feet of earth is pretty heavy.
49) They don't play Metallica in cemeteries.
50) Braces aren't biodegradable.
51) God loves you.
52) Believe it or not, your father loves you, too.
53) Spanish One would be so boring.
54) Two words: driver's license.
55) Satan isn't exactly the type of guy you want to hang out with for eternity.
56) How could you live without Twinkies?
57) You should never regret who you are, only what you have become.

Believing that I had done my best, I crawled into bed to await tomorrow's chore: saving Rion.

I waited for him at the door to Spanish the next day and handed him the paper as he walked in. I watched him from the opposite side of the room while he read the creased sheet in his lap. I waited, but he didn't look up for the entire period. After class, I approached him, concerned, but before I could say a word, his arms were around me in a tight embrace. I hugged him for a while, tears almost blinding me. He let go, and with a soft look into my eyes, he walked out of the room. No thank you was needed, his face said it all.

A week later, Rion was transferred to another school district so that he could live with his grandmother. For weeks I heard nothing, until one night the phone rang. "Sarah, is it you?" I heard the familiar voice say. Well, it was like we had never missed a day. I updated him on Ms. Canaple's new haircut, and he told me his grades were much better, and he was on the soccer team. He is even going to counseling with his dad to help them build a stronger relationship. "But do you know what the best part is?" I sensed true happiness in his voice. "I don't regret who I am, nor what I've become."

Sarah Barnett

[EDITORS' NOTE: *Rion was lucky. Everyone isn't as fortunate. If you are depressed or thinking about hurting yourself (or if you think any of your friends are in this situation),* please call for help, toll-free: **1-800-SUICIDE**. *Remember, you are not alone. People care and can help you.* **WE LOVE YOU***!!*]

My Best Friend

Mmm. Look at those eyes, crystal-blue with just a touch of green. Those long eyelashes are just reaching for me. I can feel it. Oh, my God! Is he looking over here? No, that's silly. I'm looking at him; therefore, there is no way that he'd be looking at me. I mean, that doesn't happen in my life. Or maybe he actually is! No, no, that's just my imagination playing tricks on me. Well, you never know, crazy things do . . .

"What's up, Katie?"

"Oh, hey," I replied as my best friend, Michelle, abruptly interrupted my ongoing battle of mind versus heart.

"So who have you got your eye on tonight? I see those thoughts circling around in that mind of yours. Maybe tonight you'll actually act upon them!"

"What are you talking about? I don't have any of *those* thoughts in my head, as you like to put it. I'm perfectly content to be by myself right now."

I could feel the obviousness of the lie throughout my entire body as I tried to look Michelle straight in the eyes. I'd never lied to her before, and I'm not exactly sure why I did right then. I couldn't believe that I pulled it off. I mean, that's what best friends are for, to obsess over our crushes with. But something inside me prevented me from telling her about this one. I really liked this guy and, as horrible as this sounds, I didn't want any of my friends to mess it up. Every time I even mention that I think a guy is cute, Michelle goes into full matchmaker mode and won't snap out of it until she feels she has accomplished something. Needless to say, that never happens. She makes my crush into such a big deal that I become completely nervous around the guy, and then he thinks I am a complete idiot. I wasn't about to let that happen this time.

"Well, whatever you say. Let's go talk to Tommy, he's hot!"

What did she say? Tommy?!! How did she know? I didn't even tell her this time. No! Now she's going to become little miss matchmaker again and screw things up. Maybe I'm overreacting. Maybe she just thinks Tommy is cute. No, that's terrible! We can't go after the same guy. Michelle would never be interested in Tommy. He's too short for her. Okay, nothing to worry about.

"Come on, Katie! He's walking away!" Michelle screamed as she forcefully tugged on my cute new suede jacket.

"Okay, okay, I'm comin'."

All right, so now we are approaching him. My right foot just got closer. Now my left, right, left, right. STOP THIS! I'm not in the army! It's okay. I can do this. What is the big deal about talking to a guy anyway? He's just a human like me. Oh, but he's such a beautiful human! Look at that body! I can't do this. I can't do . . .

"Hi, Tommy. How's it goin'?" *Oh, my God, I must have sounded like the biggest nerd!*

"What's up, Katie? Hey, Michelle. You girls are looking good tonight. Having fun?"

His voice is so sexy. And he said I looked good!! But he said girlssss. He can't flirt with both of us. That's not allowed." Oh, Tommy, stop it. You're so silly. Ha ha. You're tickling me."

Michelle's giggling was loud enough to interrupt all of the conversations at that party. I couldn't believe how much she was flirting with him. Even worse, he was flirting back! Here is my best friend with the guy of my dreams—even though she doesn't know that—and the guy of my dreams was rejecting me more and more by the second. I couldn't exactly pull Michelle aside and ask her to stop. That would only make things worse. She would either be mad at me for not telling her before or she wouldn't even believe me. The only thing I could do was sit there and be quiet.

The whole drive home from the party I had to listen to Michelle go on and on about how amazing Tommy is. She was completely "in love" with him.

"Did you see the way he was flirting with me? I think he likes me. We were talking for an hour and he didn't seem to be paying attention to anyone else! Aren't you happy for me?"

I had always admired Michelle for the amount of confidence she had when it came to guys. If she wanted one, she went for him. Now she just sounded arrogant, as if any guy would be stupid not to like her. I just clenched my teeth, nodded my head and kept on driving.

After what seemed like the longest car ride in human history, we finally reached Michelle's house. I dropped her off, and the second I heard the door shut I started bawling.

Why was this making me so mad? She is my best friend. I should be happy for her. But I thought this was going to be my turn. I was really going to go for Tommy and make something happen with him. Michelle doesn't like him the way I do. But it's too late to say anything. We always promised each other never to let a guy come between us. I guess this is the tester.

I was awakened the next morning with a phone call, which I thought would be Michelle calling to obsess more about Tommy.

"Hello," I said in that groggy, don't-want-to-answer-it-but-feel-I have-to kind of tone.

"Hi, Katie?" A thick male voice replied through the phone, and I knew in an instant it was Tommy!

Why is he calling me? If this is to ask for Michelle's number, then I'm gonna hang up right now. No, I have to be mature about this. I should be nice. Yeah, right, man, I don't have to be nice to anybody.

"Katie, are you there?"

"Yeah, yeah, I'm here."

"Well, how are you?"

He wants to know how I am! I'll tell him how I am! I'm a depressed teenage girl who thought she had a chance with a guy who she thought had some class. But now she finds out that this guy is in love with her best friend when he has no clue what he'd be missing by going out with her. I've been bawling and tossing all night as if I was trying to quit an addiction, and hearing his voice right now drives me even crazier because it reminds me how much I still like him.

"Oh, I'm fine, just catching up on some sleep." It's amazing how the lie seemed to shoot right out of my mouth.

"I'm sorry if I woke you. I was just calling . . . well . . . I feel kind of weird doing this . . ."

Just get it out already! I'll give you her number!

"Okay, here goes. Do you want to see a movie or something tonight? You probably think I'm really weird since we haven't even spoken that much. But you seemed really cool, and I thought I would take a chance. If you really don't want to it's okay,

I'll understand. I just thought . . ."

Oh, my God! Oh, my God! What's happening here? He's asking me *out! What happened to Michelle? This can't be right. But it is. It is! It is! It is! I have to say something now. Breathe. Calm. Act like a sane person.*

"That sounds great, Tommy. Which movie were you thinking?"

Which movie?! Why did I say that? It doesn't matter which movie we see!

"I don't know. Why don't I pick you up at seven and we'll go and see which ones are playing?"

He sounds so calm. I wonder if I sound that calm.

"Okay, great, I'll see you at seven. Bye."

"Bye."

I am going on a date with TOMMY!!! I can't believe this. This is amazing, it's incredible, it's . . . terrible! What about Michelle? She's going to kill me. I have to call her.

"Michelle, I really need to talk to you." My voice was as shaky as my body, she had to know something was up.

"What's wrong? Are you okay?" She was worried about me. Great, I'm about to hurt my best friend.

"Yeah, I'm fine. I just wanted to tell you that Tommy called me. He wanted . . ."

"He wanted my phone number, huh? I knew it!"

"Well, not exactly. He seemed kind of, well, I don't know . . . he asked me to go see a movie tonight." The words came out slower than imaginable. I thought I was about to be attacked by Michelle's raging hormones any second now. "Before you get mad, I want to explain myself, and you have to believe me."

I was completely honest with Michelle. I explained how I liked Tommy for a long time and apologized profusely for not telling her sooner. I told her about her matchmaker disease and how I had cried the whole night before. I recited my conversation with Tommy word for word and poured out a million more apologies. The weight had been lifted off my shoulders, but I felt I had just passed it on to her. The long period of silence that followed assured me that Michelle was not going to accept my apology that quickly.

After not being able to take the silence any more, I broke in and asked, "Are you all right? What are you thinking? Do you hate me? Do you want me to break my date? What? At least give me an idea of how you feel."

The heavy breathing on the other side of the phone was about to become a whimper when I heard the *click*. She didn't even say a word, just hung up. I called her back fifty times that day only to hear an answering machine that demanded that I never call her again. I have never felt so torn before in my life. The first time that something exciting actually happens to me, it has to break up the only solid relationship that I have in my life. Michelle and I always thought we were above this type of situation. Our friendship was too strong to let a boy break it up. We refused to be like those other cliques of girls that backstabbed each other all the time.

I called Tommy and explained the whole situation. He felt terrible and agreed that we could cancel our date for the night. He was disappointed but he understood. Every day for the following three weeks, I felt like I was in some never-ending chase. I would track Michelle down whenever I could and try to convince her to talk to me. I would fail each time. She would either snicker some rude comment or just shoot me down or she wouldn't say anything at all. I never realized she had the ability to be so cruel. After the countless number of rejections, I slowly began to give up. I couldn't keep chasing after something that she seemed to have given up on a long time ago. It was too frustrating and disappointing.

Tommy was great throughout the whole ordeal. We continued to see each other and became extremely close. I could safely say he was my best friend. As for Michelle, her hostility toward me slowly began to wear down but we still weren't friends. We had one of those say-hi-to-each-other-in-the-hallway relationships. The pain of losing her friendship never diminished either. I would find myself suddenly crying sometimes when I would think of what happened to our relationship. I wondered if she ever even missed me.

About a week ago, eight months after everything had happened, I built up the courage to ask Michelle if she wanted to go out to lunch with me. To my ultimate surprise, she agreed. We spent most of the lunch having little chit-chat conversations about the things happening in our lives. The whole time I wanted to scream at her about how much I missed her. I wanted to go back to my house, change into our pajamas, and gossip about every little detail about every little thing that could possibly be gossiped about! I wanted to laugh with her and feel comfortable around her. I wanted to curl up and eat five scoops of Häagen-Dazs coffee chip ice cream while we watched our favorite movies that we've both seen 50 million times. Most of all, I wanted the security of knowing that I had my best friend back.

The meaningless chit-chat continued until I reached Michelle's house to drop her off. The last time I had dropped Michelle off I had wanted to strangle her for obsessing over Tommy so much. Now all I wanted to do was hug her so tight so that she could never leave me again. Fortunately, I didn't have to. As I pulled the car over to the curb, Michelle looked at me with her welcoming warm eyes and said the four words that brought my whole eight months of misery to an end, "I've really missed you!"

Tears began to fall down my face but no words would come out. I looked into her eyes, leaned forward and gave my best friend a big hug.

Lisa Rothbard

Healing with Love

Nobody's family can hang out the sign, "Nothing the matter here."

CHINESE PROVERB

On a bitterly cold and cloudy winter's day in upstate New York, I saw my brother again for the first time in a year. As my father and I pulled up to the reform school after four hours of driving, his attempts at cheerful commentary did nothing to ameliorate the dismal apprehension that I felt. I had little hope that my brother would be changed and, furthermore, I had convinced myself that any appearance of change would not necessarily be genuine.

Being with my brother after so long was

like getting to know him all over again. Over the next couple of days, I felt a kind of peace developing between us, and, for the first time, I wasn't tense around him, nor was I scared of what he would do or say next. It seemed as though I would finally find a friend in my brother, and, more than that, I would find a true brother in my brother. While part of me rejoiced in his transformation, another part of me thought it was too good to be true, and so I remained skeptical of his seeming progress. Two days was surely not enough time to erase the hostility that had built up between us over the years. I showed this cynical front to my father and brother, while the hopeful voice remained hidden deep inside of my heart, afraid to appear, lest it should be trampled upon. My brother himself commented several times on my depressed disposition, but I knew he would never understand the complexity of my feelings, so I remained elusive.

I wrapped myself in this same protective silence during, what was for me, the most emotionally trying part of the visit. Meals at the school were more than just meals. They were chaperoned with two teachers at each table, and provided a forum for judging the students' progress and/or continued delinquency. My father had told me that these meals often lasted for an hour or two, as each student was treated separately and with the full attention of the table. As we sat down for lunch, I knew I wouldn't be able to make it through the meal without crying.

Several boys and girls were "brought up" in front of the table for transgressions they had committed, but a boy named Brian touched me the most. A fairly new arrival at the school, he hadn't yet lost the initial anger and bitterness at having been brought there against his will. He was an attractive boy, about sixteen years old and was, my father whispered to me, an exceptional soccer player with a promising future in the sport. As the head teacher at our table conducted a heavy interrogation of him, Brian shifted his weight nervously every two seconds, and I saw in his eyes what I had become so good at reading in my brother's. They darted anxiously about the room, resting upon everything except the man addressing him, and I knew that he was searching for someone or something to blame. He wasn't yet aware that only when he stopped looking for excuses could he truly hear and learn from those trying to help him.

Suddenly, out of the corner of my eye, I became aware of a bearded man standing at the closed door and peering in apprehensively at our solemn gathering, which must have looked more like an AA meeting than a meal. The realization that it was Brian's father trying to catch a glimpse of his son precipitated the first tear I had shed all weekend.

"Why is Brian here?" I whispered softly to my father.

"Oh, you know, the usual, drugs, violence . . . I think the last straw was when he hit his father in the head with one of his soccer trophies. . . . He was chosen for the National All-Star team, you know. . . . Must be quite a player."

As the tears flowed more freely down my face, Brian looked straight ahead at the wall and told us that he had refused to see his father who had driven for many hours to see him.

Then the teacher spoke, "Brian, I talked to your dad, and he says he brought you your puppy because he knows how much you must miss him. He's willing to accept the fact that you don't want to see him, but he wants you to know that you can see your puppy."

I was screaming inside. I wanted to stand up and tell Brian how lucky he was to have a father who obviously loved him so much, and who loved him enough to do the hardest thing a parent ever has to do: send his child away. I was bursting to enlighten him, but I knew it was something he would have to learn on his own, so I remained still and just let the overwhelming sadness spread over me like a dark cloud.

That afternoon, I saw my brother waving good-bye as we pulled up the dirt drive and out of the gates of the school. I couldn't look back, as I was too busy trying to suppress the emotion that I felt creeping up on me with the force of a tidal wave. I was filled with hopelessness and empathy for these kids who had somehow gotten lost along the way. I knew there was a fine line between them and me, a line I had walked like a tightrope at several times in my life.

Indeed, part of my sadness lay in the guilt I felt for not having such a heavy load to bear and for never being able to fully comprehend the nature and sheer weight of this load my brother carried.

Several months later I returned to the school, this time in early spring and accompanied by my whole family, including my mother and two sisters. Everything looked brighter and more colorful in the sun. Wildflowers bloomed on the hillside looking out over the valley, and the water in the pond sparkled like jewels. I closed my eyes, held my face up to the sun and smiled. It was my family's first reunion in over a year. As it was family weekend, everywhere I looked I saw proud, attentive parents and beaming kids. This is when the full force of what I was experiencing hit me. For the first time in a while, I didn't feel the despair and hopelessness of these kids' lives, but the tremendous amount of love and support that surrounded each one of them. After a whole year spent doubting that my brother would ever be able to function normally in society, I allowed the seeds of hope to germinate in my mind, as well as in my heart.

Moments later, my new outlook was strengthened and forever cemented by the most beautiful sight I think I have ever seen. At first I couldn't believe my eyes. Brian and his father were walking arm in arm across the grass towards the pond and seemed to be in quiet discussion about one of those everyday, mundane things that is the business of fathers and their sons. A golden retriever, now fully grown, wagged its tail in delight as he trotted after them.

Cecile Wood

Ghost Mother

If you cannot get rid of the family skeleton, you may as well make it dance.

George Bernard Shaw

Six months before my thirteenth birthday, my parents gave my brother and me "the talk." The one about their loving us, but not each other and how much happier everyone would be if they separated. Yet, my parents rewrote the ending: "We think it would be best if you lived with your father." My mother was the one who said this, running her red nails through my hair. That moment has stayed in the center of my stomach since then, like a jagged stone rolling around.

Mothers are supposed to be that one

person who represents home, who somehow makes everything okay when your world is shaking. A mother should be there for you no matter how many times you change your Halloween costume, how messy your room gets or what happens to her marriage. But mine saw motherhood as an optional endeavor, something she could easily discard like a sweater that no longer fit.

She quickly settled into her own life and her new apartment. Having married at twenty-one, this was the first time she was on her own. Her decorating business was growing, and she was more interested in catering to her clients than to two kids and a husband of fifteen years.

A few weeks after she moved out, she called on a Friday night. "Tomorrow, let's have lunch and then go shopping. Okay?" she asked. I was so excited that I could hardly answer. That night I dreamed of riding beside my mom in the car. Saturday, I woke early, put on my favorite overalls and finished my homework in case she wanted to spend Sunday together, too. My friend Jennifer called. "Aren't you coming to the movies?" she asked. "Everyone's going."

"My mom and I have stuff to do. Shopping or something," I said, forcing my tone to be matter-of-fact. But morning turned into afternoon, and she didn't call. I spent the day by the phone pretending to read, playing solitaire and braiding my hair. I wouldn't eat anything because I thought at any minute she'd be there and want to take me out for lunch. And I didn't want my mom to have to eat alone. But she didn't call until after six o'clock. "Sorry, honey, I was working all day and not near a phone," she said quickly. "And now I'm so tired, I just need to take a nap. You understand, don't you?" No Mom, I didn't understand.

This same scenario happened many weekends for several years after she left. The rare times I did see her, she'd rent me four-hour movies like *Tess* and leave me alone to watch them. Or I'd go on her errands or to her office, never really with her, more like a balloon trailing after her. I'd sit alone at a desk in her office eating Chinese food out of a paper carton while she worked or talked on the phone. But I never complained or stopped going. How could I when this was all I had of her?

Almost a year after she moved out, the clothes she didn't want remained in her walk-in closet. My father said he was too busy to pack them, but I think that—just as I did—he hoped it meant she wasn't gone for good. I used to sit in that closet, breathing in the lingering smell of her Ralph Lauren perfume. I'd wrap myself in her ivory cashmere cardigan and run my fingers along the beaded surface of a pink bag, remembering when she'd carried it with a chiffon dress. She had looked just like a princess. I'd rock the bag gently, feeling sorry for it that she had left it behind, too.

Living with my father and brother in their masculine world of boxer shorts and hockey games wasn't easy. Just when I should have been stepping out of my tomboy stage of wearing my brother's worn Levi's and button-downs and starting to become a young woman, I was screaming at the basketball players on TV and munching on Doritos. Each of my friends watched her mother apply eyeliner and blush and practiced with her makeup while she was out. The only makeup I knew about was the black smudges under football players' eyes.

Growing up without my mother, I always

had to carry myself to each new stage of life or get left behind. I wore the same clothes that my friends did, bought my first bra by myself and started shaving my legs when they did. But to me I was just following clumsily behind them, self-conscious that my motherlessness was showing. When I got my period, I huddled in my pink bathroom, feeling like a little girl at this sign of being a woman. Having to say, "I got my period, Dad," was mortifying. But the truth was, I felt more comfortable telling him than my mother. When she called the following week, she said, "Dad told me what happened, but he took care of it." This was a statement, not a question.

My mother became like a distant relative whom I saw several times a year, who sent a birthday card if she remembered and to whom I was stiffly polite and didn't curse in front of. The word "mom" was foreign to me. She never asked about my friends or school or seemed to notice that I was struggling to grow up without her. Each time I said good-bye, I knew it would be months before I saw her again.

Why didn't my mother want me? I wondered. Teachers and friends' parents always wore a look of pity when my father picked me up from parties, came alone to plays and parent conference day and talked to them to arrange car pools. Hating their pity, I'd mix the few minutes my mother did give me with my imagination. Then I'd casually talk about her at lunch or at friends' houses so they wouldn't see that all I had was a ghost mother who touched my life only in memories.

Although it was tough at first, my father tried to do everything he could to fill the gaps my mother left. He put my brother and me first, at times sacrificing his own happiness for ours. Despite losing his wife and marriage, my father wore a smile on his face. After all, he was the person we looked toward to tell us everything was going to be okay, so we couldn't see him sad. He had no spouse to pick up where he left off or to help him with daily issues and unexpected situations. He took us to the doctor, listened to our problems and helped us with homework. He was there with treats when my friends slept over and told the kind of dumb fatherly jokes that made us laugh and roll our eyes. He was always at all my school plays and softball games. He never missed a gymnastics meet or recital. Most fathers never took off work to come to even one of these things; my father was at all of them.

Most of all, he was always conscious of my disappointments and tried to make a bad situation better. After a while, all the people who pitied me noticed my father's intense interest in my well-being and realized, as I did, that though my life was different, there was nothing wrong with it or me. In time, I adjusted to this. And though I never stopped wishing my mother were a more central part of my life, I saw the fact that she wasn't; she was just a part of who I am.

In recent years, I have become closer with her. I accept her for who she is, regardless of the fact that she wasn't always the mother I wanted her to be. As I have gotten older, I can look at what she did from a different perspective. And I think I've reached this point because my father taught me to be understanding of and sensitive to others. I've realized it's okay not to have a storybook home with a mom, dad, two kids and a dog. Who said that is the definition of family? My home may have been unique, but it had in it the same love and loyalty as other families.

Michele Bender

Terri Jackson

It is easy to laugh; it is so easy to hurt; it takes strength to be kind and gentle.

ANONYMOUS

On the first day of sixth grade, I sat in my quiet homeroom class and observed all the people who I would eventually befriend and possibly graduate with. I glanced around the room and noticed that the majority of the middle-class kids were dressed in their nicest first-day outfits. My glance stopped on a shy-looking girl in the back of the room. She wore a stained, yellow plaid shirt with a pair of frayed jeans that had obviously had several owners before her. Her hair was unusually short and unwashed.

She wore dress shoes that were once white, and frilly pink socks that had lost their frill with too many wearings. I caught myself thinking, "That's disgusting. Doesn't she know what a bathtub is?" As I looked around, I figured others were probably thinking the same thing.

The teacher began checking the attendance, each person casually lifting his or her hand as names were called in turn.

"Terri Jackson?" the teacher asked, following the roll with her finger. Silence. "Um, Terri Jackson?"

Finally we heard a meek answer from the back of the room, followed by the sound of ripping cloth. We all shifted in our seats to see what had happened.

"Scary Terri ripped the armpit of her shirt!" one boy joked.

"Eww, I bet it's a hundred years old!" another girl commented. One comment after another brought a roar of laugher.

I was probably laughing the loudest. Sadly, making Terri feel insecure made me feel secure and confident. It was a good break from the awkward silence and uncomfortable first-day jitters.

Terri Jackson was the joke of the whole sixth grade that year. If we had nothing to talk about, Terri's trip through the lunchroom was an entertaining conversation starter. Her grandma-looking dress, missing front tooth and stained gym clothes kept us mocking and imitating her for hours.

At my twelfth birthday party, ten giggly, gossipy girls were playing Truth or Dare, a favorite party game. We had just finished a Terri Jackson discussion. It was my turn at the game.

"Umm . . . Sydney! Truth or Dare?" one of my friends asked.

"How about a dare? Bring it on. I'll do anything." Oh, if only I'd known what she was about to say.

"Okay, I dare you to invite Terri Jackson over to your house next Friday for two whole hours!"

"Two whole hours?! Please ask something else, *please*!" I begged. "How could anybody do that?" But my question was drowned out by a sea of giggly girls slapping their hands over their mouths and rolling on the floor, trying to contain their laughter.

The next day, I cautiously walked up to

Terri as if her body odor was going to make me fall over dead. My friends huddled and watched from a corner to see if I would follow through with the brave dare.

I managed to choke out, "Hey Scary—I mean Terri—you want to come over for two hours Friday?" I didn't see her face light up because I had turned to my friends and made a gagging expression. When I was satisfied with their laughter of approval, I turned back to Terri. Terri's face was buried in her filthy hands; she was crying. I couldn't stand it. Half of me felt the strongest compassion for her, but the other half wanted to slap her for making me look so cruel and heartless. That was exactly what I was being.

"What's got you all upset? All I did was invite you over," I whispered, trying not to show my concern.

She looked up and watched my eyes for what seemed like forever. "Really?" That was all she could say. Her seldom-heard voice almost startled me.

"I guess so, if you're up to it." My voice sounded surprisingly sincere. I'd never seen her flash her toothless smile so brightly. The rest of the day I had a good feeling, and I was not dreading the two-hour visit as I had before. I was almost looking forward to it.

Friday rolled around quickly. My time with Terri passed by in a flash as the two hours slipped into four hours, and I found myself actually enjoying her company. We chatted about her family and her battles with poverty. We discovered that we both played violin, and my favorite part of the afternoon occurred when she played the violin for me. I was amazed by how beautifully she played.

I would love to tell you that Terri and I became best friends and that from then on I ignored all my other friends' comments. But that's not how it happened. While I no longer participated in the Terri bashings and even tried to defend her at times, I didn't want to lose everyone else's acceptance just to gain Terri's.

Terri disappeared after the sixth grade. No one is sure what happened to her. We think that she may have transferred to a different school because of how cruelly the kids treated her. I still think about her sometimes and wonder what she's doing. I guess all I can do is hope that she is being accepted and loved wherever she is.

I realize now how insecure and weak I was during that sixth-grade year. I participated in the cruel, heartless Terri-bashing sessions because they seemed kind of funny in a distorted way. But they were only funny because they falsely boosted my own self-confidence; I felt bigger by making someone else feel smaller. I know now that true confidence is not proven by destroying another's self-esteem, but rather, by having the strength to stand up for the Terri Jacksons of the world.

Sydney Fox

A Name in the Sand

The influence of each human being on others in this life is a kind of immortality.

John Quincy Adams

I sit on the rocky edge of a boulder, letting my feet dangle in the stillness of the water, and gaze out at the rippling waves crawling into shore like an ancient sea turtle. A salty mist hangs above the water, and I can feel it gently kissing my face. I lick my lips and can taste the familiar presence of salt from the ocean water. Above my head seagulls circle, searching the shallow, clear water for food and calling out to one another. And in my hand rests. . . .

The sound of a hospital bed being rolled

down the hallway outside my mother's hospital room brought me out of my daydreams. The ocean was gone and all that was left was a bare hospital room, its only decorations consisting of flowers, cards and seashells carefully arranged on a table next to my mother's bed.

My mother was diagnosed with cancer about a year ago, a year full of months spent in various hospitals, radiation therapy, doses of chemotherapy and other methods to try to kill the cancer eating away at her life. But the tumors keep growing and spreading, and all the treatments have done is weaken her already frail body. The disease is now in its final course and, although nobody has told me, I know my mother won't be coming home this time.

I tried to change my thoughts, and they once again returned to my daydreams. Everything seemed so clear and so real, the sound of the waves, the taste of salt, the seagulls, and the . . . what was in my hand? I glanced down at my hands and realized I was holding my mother's favorite shell. I placed it against my ear, and the sound of the ocean sent cherished memories crashing into my mind.

Every year, my mother, my father and I would spend our summer vacations in a little cabin down by the ocean. As a little girl, I would explore this stretch of sand with my parents. Walking hand-in-hand, they would swing me high into the air as we ran to meet the incoming surf. And it was there, in those gentle waves, where my parents first taught me how to swim. I would wear my favorite navy blue-and-white striped swimsuit, and my father's strong arms would support me, while my mother's gentle hands would guide me through the water. After many mouthfuls of swallowed salty ocean water I could swim by myself, while my parents stood close by, proudly and anxiously watching over me. And it was in those grains of sand, not on a piece of paper that could be saved and displayed on a refrigerator, that I first painstakingly wrote my name.

My family's fondest memories weren't captured on film and put in a photo album, but were captured in the sand, wind and water of the ocean. Last summer was the final time my family would ever go to the ocean all together. This summer was nearly over and had been filled with memories of various hospitals, failed treatments, false hopes, despair, sorrow and tears.

I glanced over at my mother lying in her hospital bed, peacefully asleep after the doctor had given her some medicine for her pain. I wanted to cry out to God, "Why, why my mother? How can I live without her to help me through my life? Don't take her away from my father and me!" My tears and sobs began to fade away, as the dripping of my mother's IV hypnotized me into a restless sleep.

* * * *

"Ashes to ashes, and dust to dust," droned the pastor, while my father and I spread my mother's ashes over the ocean water. Some of them fell into the water and dissolved, while others were caught in the wind and carried away. This was my mother's final wish—to be in the place she loved the most, where all her favorite memories live on.

As the funeral concluded and people began to drift away saying words of comfort to my father and me, I stayed behind to say my final farewell to Mother. I carried her favorite shell that brought her so much comfort while she was in the hospital and unable to hear the sounds of the ocean. I put it to my ear and the sound of the ocean seemed almost muted. I looked into the shell and was surprised to find a piece of paper stuck inside of it. I pulled the paper out and read its words:

To my daughter, I will always love you
and be with you.
A name in the sand will never last,
The waves come rolling into shore high
and fast.
And wash the lines away,
But not the memories we shared that day.
Where we have trod this sandy shore,
Our traces we left there will be no more.
But, wherever we are,
The memories will never be far.
Although I may not be with you,
Know that my love for you will always
be true.
Those memories will last forever,
And in them we shall always be together.

Hold them close to your heart,
And know that from your side
I will never part.

As I crossed the beach, I stooped and wrote my mother's name in the sand. I continued onward, turning only to cast one last lingering look behind, and the waves had already begun to wash my lines away.

Elizabeth Stumbo

Inner Sustenance

All of the significant battles are waged within the self.

Sheldon Kopp

All I ever wanted was to be popular. Have the coolest friends. Be in a hot rock band and date the best-looking men—simple wishes for a young girl. Some of my dreams even came true. I started a rock band. And the cutest guy at Melbourne High School even asked me out.

I answered yes of course, but within a week, he complained, "Your hips are too big. You need to lose weight to look thin like the other girls in your band."

Immediately, I tried several different diets

to lose weight. For one, I ate grapefruit and vegetables only. That didn't work; I felt faint and had to eat. The second week I tried skipping breakfast and dinner. When I did that, I became so hungry by the time dinner came, I splurged and eventually started gaining weight. Ten pounds I added in a month trying to please my boyfriend. Instead of praising my efforts, he cut me down even more. "You look like a whale," he said, making me feel not as pretty as my other friends who wanted to date him. I felt self-conscious and didn't want to lose him as a boyfriend, so I desperately searched for another way to lose the pounds that were keeping him at bay.

I didn't even think that he was the problem: just me, it was just me. Whatever I ate made me fatter. Whatever I wore, I looked hideous. I was now 110 pounds, a complete blimp!

One evening after a date, I got so angry by his "whale" remarks that I ate an enormous piece of cake. The guilt made me want to try something I had seen other girls in my school doing at lunch break: throw up. I went to my bathroom and without even thinking of the consequences, stuck my finger down my throat and threw up in the toilet.

All I ever wanted was to be as pretty as a model. I wanted my boyfriend to look at me the same way as he did those bikini-poster girls.

It was so easy. That cake I just enjoyed didn't cost me any unwanted calories.

Once a day soon turned into three forced vomits. Becoming malnourished, I was constantly hungry, so I ate more, threw up more. It wasn't until I strangely gained another fifteen pounds and tried to quit a month later that I realized I couldn't stop. I fought to, for several weeks. As soon as I got up from the table, my stomach began convulsing. Now my own stomach somehow believed that's what it was supposed to do. I had to run from the table. I was throwing up without even sticking my finger down my throat or even wanting to!

I wasn't in control anymore. I was caught in a whirlwind. I thought bulimia would help me lose pounds but after the months of doing it, not only hadn't it controlled my weight, but the purging had opened up the pits of hell.

I needed help. My boyfriend's comments and my weight were the least of my problems now and I knew it. At age fifteen I didn't know what to do. Desperate for a solution, I broke down into tears and confided in the only person I could trust: my mom. Unsure, of how she would react and wondering if she'd stop loving me if she knew, I mustered up the courage to write the truth on a note and leave it on her dresser:

"Mom, I'm sick. I tried forcing myself to throw up to lose weight, now I am vomiting every day. I can't stop. I'm afraid I'm going to die."

I locked myself in my room the entire night. My mother knocked on my door several times. I could hear her crying. The next morning she pounded harder and told me she had made a doctor's appointment for me. "Get out here before we're late!" she said.

I opened the door. Instead of a hard and loud scolding, I received a hug. Being in her understanding arms, I had the confidence to go to the doctor with her.

The first meeting with the doctor, I'll

never forget. He told me that by using bulimia to lose weight I was actually retaining water, losing hair, ruining the enamel on my teeth and was now developing a very serious stomach condition called gastritis. He informed me I was malnourished and in danger of losing my life. He strongly recommended that I check myself into a hospital for treatment.

Knowing that I would be apart from my friends and my mother, I didn't want to agree. Going to the hospital seemed to be a way of walking away from everything I've ever known. I was terrified about leaving home. I'd never been away from my house, my school or my friends before. I was wondering if anyone would even stay my friend or if they all would think I was a freak. I thought about telling the doctor I wouldn't even consider it, but my conscience reminded me, *If I don't go I'll be spending the rest of my days, however many more I have left, throwing my life away, literally down the toilet.* I told the doctor I would go.

The first day and night were the hardest. Nurses gave me a study schedule for both educational and counseling activities. I would attend six different classes each day: math, English, science, group counseling, PE and a personal session with my doctor. All the people were complete strangers. Most of the patients my age weren't there for eating disorders but for severe mental illnesses or violent behaviors. In my first class, math, I sat down and said hello to the girl sitting next to me. She turned her head and ignored me. I shifted in my chair and waved to the girl on my left and asked what her problem was. She didn't answer and mumbled something about needing medicine. I quickly learned that the other patients were hard to relate to or on heavy medication. They didn't seem to have any desire to make friends. That night, I cried myself to sleep, feeling more alone than I ever had.

The next morning, I was told that my blood work reported that I was not only dehydrated but also starving. The doctor said he wouldn't release me until I was strong inside and out. Months passed like this and I continued attending classes with screaming, irrational kids. I felt so isolated. The doctors tried several types of medicines; none of them seemed to be working to keep my food down. They started feeding me intravenously. A needle was stuck in the top of my hand and stayed there, taped, twenty-four hours a day. It was so gross, having a big needle sticking out in my hand. Every morning they would attach a liquid-filled bag that dripped nutrients into my bloodstream. Each night they gave me pills that made me nauseous and want to throw up. I was becoming more and more discouraged. *Will I ever be normal again?* I wondered. Still, I wouldn't give up. I knew what I had to do and I tried yet another medication.

When that didn't seem to do anything, a nurse came into my room, took that morning's medication out of my hand and suggested that I stand in front of the mirror one hour after each meal and repeat to myself these words, "Yes, I am perfect because God made me."

I thought she was nuts! If modern medicine couldn't work, how could saying a few words do the trick? Still, I knew I had to try it. It couldn't hurt and if it got me off the feeding tube, it was worth it no matter how crazy it sounded. Beside, if it didn't work, I could tell the nurse that it wasn't the cure and that at least I tried.

The next meal, I said the words for several minutes. Religiously. I said them for an entire week extending the time every day. After a while, I realized I began saying them as if I meant them and I had been keeping my food down. My bulimia was becoming under control because my mind stopped focusing on throwing up, and started focusing on saying those words! Within a week I stopped needing to be fed through tubes, my stomach had stopped rejecting food and my compulsion to vomit ceased. My mind had been tricked into more positive thinking!

With the support of my counselors and nurses, I continued searching for ways to bolster my self-esteem, so that I would never again be so vulnerable to the judgments of others. I began to read self-esteem books and the Bible to further my self-image. By then, my boyfriend had dumped me. Most of my friends had stopped coming to see me. Even on the day I celebrated my newfound ability to keep my food down, I called my brother to tell him the good news and he said, "You're making all this up for attention, aren't you?"

I can't tell you how much that hurt. Still,

I wouldn't let the outside world's cruelty diminish my victory or my newly found self-esteem of loving myself no matter what my weight was. Finally, I realized with this new strength, I was well.

I began feeding myself and choosing to be full—literally, spiritually, emotionally and physically. My self-esteem strengthened as I ate, repeated those words, and learned to love myself. By gulping down food, I became the vessel God had created me to be. I was special regardless of what others thought. And, I saw that old boyfriend for what he really was: shallow, close-minded, inconsiderate, and not even worthy of my love in the first place.

It had taken months in the hospital with nurses and counseling to learn a lesson I'll never forget. Being popular is just an illusion. If you love yourself you are in the "in" crowd. You are an individual gift from God to the world. It's comforting to know joy comes from being who I am instead of trying to become somebody else's perfect model.

My first day back to school, my ex-boyfriend actually came up to me and asked me out again. "Wow, you look great. You're so thin! You want to go to the football game on Friday?"

"No," I answered, without regret. "I'd rather date someone who loves my heart."

Me! Accepting me suddenly became a daily celebration of life. I love me! Those three words sound so simple, but living them, believing them makes living so tantalizingly delicious!

Michelle Wallace Campanelli

Center Stage

Answer that you are here - that life exists and identity, that the powerful play goes on, and you may contribute a verse.

Walt Whitman

Once upon a time, my life was as orderly as the inside of my locker. I took detailed notes, never talked out of turn, helped put away library books during my free periods, and went to track practice after school. But all that changed the day Mr. Soames made Sara McGee my partner in biology.

"If he thinks I'm touching this, he's dreaming," Sara whispered after Mr. Soames told us to make the first incision into the earthworms we were dissecting. She pushed her bangs—

they were orange today as opposed to last week's green—out of her face and frowned.

I took the knife from her hand and split the earthworm neatly down its center.

"Thanks," she said. She rolled up her sleeves and her silver bangles clattered. "I know I'm a baby, but cutting open animals makes me sick."

I finished dissecting the worm, and when the period was over, Sara slipped her backpack over her shoulder and asked me to eat lunch with her.

"Okay," I said, surprised. I followed her to her locker, where she opened a tube of tomato-red lipstick and thickly applied it.

"Want some?" she asked, but I shook my head "no."

"Just a tiny bit?" she asked again, and before I could stop her, she dabbed it on. Then she removed the tortoise-shell barrette I always wore and lifted my hair into a high ponytail, pulling two tendrils down on either side of my ears.

"Stunning!" she said, standing behind me so that I could see both of us in the little mirror that hung from a hook. Stunning? I wasn't so sure.

Soon, whenever Sara chewed Juicy Fruit gum in class, I did, too, even though I was careful not to get caught. I wore long skirts like Sara's, and dangle earrings. She hid in the stacks during study hall and read old magazines and, consequently, so did I. She took me to Papa Jimmy's and introduced me to double caffé lattes and biscotti dipped in chocolate. She liked to start arguments in world history class about personal freedom and even though I never could do that, I did find myself, miraculously, volunteering to read out loud in Mr. Bernard's English class.

It was Mr. Bernard, in fact, who pulled me aside and told me I had a flair for drama (we were reading *Romeo and Juliet*). He also said I should try out for the part of Laura in the junior class production of *The Glass Menagerie*.

"No way. I could never do that," I told Sara as soon as we left the room. Secretly, though, I was pleased he had asked.

"Of course you can. You'll be great," Sara said. "You have to try out!" She bugged me until I finally agreed.

At the audition, I read a scene with Joe Greenlaw, who I'd never said a word to before. I doubt he knew who I was, but I could recite his activities as if they were listed in alphabetical order under his picture in the yearbook: junior class vice-president; photo editor for the Park Ridge *Banner*; captain, debate team; soccer goalie.

After we finished, Mrs. Layton, the director, just smiled and said, "Thank you *very* much," and the next day the casting list was posted on the bulletin board and there was my name, second from the top, with Joe Greenlaw's just above it.

I had play rehearsal almost every night, and so I had to use all my free time to catch up on my schoolwork and hardly ever had time to go to Papa Jimmy's with Sara. Slowly, though, a strange thing began to happen. Homework and chores, babysitting, and even Sara started to fade in importance, but the time I spent at rehearsals was as vivid as the glow-in-the-dark stars on my bedroom ceiling.

Joe talked to me, calling "Laura" from way down the hall. This made me so happy that I didn't even mind when I saw Rachel Thompson, who had waist-long hair that was shiny as glass, put her arm across his shoulder. One night, during dress rehearsal week, we were standing together on the fire escape outside the auditorium watching the snow flakes gather on the iron railing. Joe told me that deep down inside he was really shy and that he was glad he could be himself with me. "Maybe we should do things together," he said. "Go running, go to a dance, I don't know." And then we heard Mrs. Layton calling for us, so we ran back inside.

The next day, Sara stood by my locker just before homeroom. "Hi," she said.

"Hi."

"I never see you anymore. Except in classes, and that doesn't count." She tugged on one of the four stud earrings that lined her ear.

"I know," I said. "It's the play. I'm really busy. It'll be over soon." I looked closely at Sara, past her makeup, and her jewelry, and the long black cape that covered her shirt and her thick, black hiking boots. She always seemed so bold, the way she stated her opinions as if they were facts, and looked anybody in the eye. But now she was quiet, more like the old me than Sara. I gave her a hug.

"Let's do something," she suggested. She looked at the poster on the bulletin board just behind us. It was a drawing of a flapper girl twirling a strand of pearls. "Let's get a bunch of people together and crash the Winter Carnival dance. We'll go to the thrift shop and get some beaded dresses."

A dance. I thought of Joe and of our conversation the night before. And even though I knew, deep down, that it would be a white lie to say he'd invited me to that particular dance, I told her I was busy. "I can't," I said. She looked at me and waited. "Joe Greenlaw asked me."

"Yeah, right," she said.

"I'm sorry," I told her. "He did." Sara picked up her backpack from between her feet and started to walk away.

"Sara!" I called after her.

"Let me know when you can fit me into your busy schedule," she hissed.

* * * *

This is the part of my story that is really embarrassing—the part that I wish I could tell in third person, as if it really belonged to somebody else. A week after the play was over Joe found me during sixth-period study hall. "I'm sorry," he said.

I looked at him, not understanding.

"Sara McGee asked me if it was true we were going to the dance together. I'm sorry. I'm going with Rachel."

I looked down at my feet. The new me was going away, like a picture on a computer screen that fades out. I was sure my ears were bright red.

"I'm sorry," Joe continued. "It's nothing personal." He turned and looked like he was leaving, but then he came back. He put his hand on my arm. "Don't be embarrassed," he said. "You know, I should have asked you. I wish I had." And then he left.

Now Sara passed me in the hall without speaking. I spent most of my free time studying or practicing my sprints. I went back to wearing my plain, comfortable clothes and threw away my makeup. And I only talked when teachers called on me. As if nothing had changed.

But that wouldn't be true. To Sara, I might have looked the same. Still, deep inside, where she couldn't see, there was another me. I was brave, I was fun. I got a standing ovation in the middle of a stage, and a boy regretted not asking me to a dance. And it was Sara I had to thank for introducing that girl to me.

Jane Denitz Smith

Finding a Vision

Face your deficiencies and acknowledge them; but do not let them master you. Let them teach you patience, sweetness, insight.

HELEN KELLER

Six years ago, I went blind. Due to a severe herpes simplex virus in my eyes, I lost one of my most precious possessions: my eyesight. Tiny cold sores covered the surface of my eyes, scarring my cornea. I wasn't allowed to stand in direct sunlight or even in a brightly lit room. The light would penetrate my eyelids and cause too much pain. At the age of seventeen, I was unprepared to find myself in a dark world. Who would I be without my ability to see?

All I wanted throughout the entire summer was to be able to see people. What new cute bathing suit styles was everyone wearing? Who had cut their hair or dyed it purple? I would have a conversation with someone and realize that I had no idea what facial expressions he was making. I no longer had the ability to make eye contact, a privilege I had taken for granted before. I longed to talk with my eyes. I just wasn't whole without my vision.

My parents became my sole support system. Hoping for a miracle, they took me to an eye specialist every day. No one was sure if I would ever completely recover, and if so, how long the healing process would take. Meanwhile, Mom and Dad adjusted their own lives in order to keep my spirits up. They would take me to baseball games and out to dinner—anything to get me out of the house. However, going places was difficult. I had to wear eye patches and dark sunglasses to ease the pain of bright light. As a seventeen-year-old, this wasn't exactly the fashion statement I was trying to make.

My parents had to take care of me everywhere. At restaurants they ordered my food, arranged it on the table, and then explained where everything was on my plate so I could finally eat it. My fifteen-year-old brother took this opportunity to rearrange the food on my plate. My mom was amazing. Each day she would brush my hair and lay out a decent looking outfit so I could walk out of the house with a little bit of pride. She was determined to keep my self-esteem as high as possible. I relied on my mom to make me feel pretty. At an age when I should have been gaining my independence, I found myself becoming increasingly dependent on my parents.

I wasn't able to drive or visit my friends. Movies were completely out of the question. Life seemed to just go on without me, as if I was never there. Fortunately, I had a wonderful friend who knew how to make me feel special. Donny and I had dated a couple of times before I lost my vision, but at that time we were just friends. He would come to my house to sit and talk with me. If the TV were on, he'd watch and I'd listen. One time, Donny took me to a baseball barbecue and introduced me to all of his friends. I had never been so happy in my entire life. He didn't care that I couldn't see his friends. He held my hand proudly and led me around. I may not have been able to see all the people I met that day, but their voices are clear in mind. I can still separate whose laughter belonged to whom. When I close my eyes now and try to remember that day, I mostly see darkness. But I can still smell the sausage and brisket cooking on the grill. I can hear the happiness around me and Donny's voice saying, "This is my girlfriend, Talina."

I slowly began to make progress toward the end of the summer. Little by little, I was able to open my eyes. My vision was still blurred but this achievement called for a celebration. My parents were still concerned and Donny continued to stay by my side. Then I began to worry, *Will I have to start my senior year wearing my thick glasses that everyone still refers to as Coke bottles?* I didn't want to think about it. August crept up on me, though, and I started school with limited vision and thick glasses. As I walked through the halls, I struggled to look confident. I had a harder time cheering at pep rallies and football games. My lack of clear vision and concern with my physical appearance took the fun out of everything that I used to love. My level of self-confidence had diminished to an unrecognizable point.

At a time in my life when I expected my only concern to be to have fun, I was learning a powerful lesson. I could no longer rely on appearance to make me feel better about myself. I had to go deeper. With the support of my family and friends, I realized that feeling good about who I am on the inside is far more important. Believing that I can overcome the obstacles that I face is crucial. My identity wasn't my thick glasses. My identity was my inner strength. This inner strength allowed me to love life even when I was unable to see it. Losing my eyesight could not take away my ability to hear the voices of the people who love me. It could not steal away the fresh smell of morning or the lingering aroma of my mom's cooking. Most important, my loss could never take from me the feel of my boyfriend's hand around my own.

Six years later, I continue to need steroid eyedrops to keep the virus from reoccurring. The scar tissue is slowly improving.

Recently, I began to wear both contacts, which is a huge accomplishment. A day doesn't go by that I am not thankful for my progress and the lesson I learned. I am incredibly thankful for my special friend who visited me, introduced me as his girlfriend and is now my husband.

I am currently preparing for my first year of teaching. I think about which of my personal qualities I might be able to share with my students. I know how difficult it is to grow up and I want my students to believe that I understand them. If I can't teach them anything else, I hope I can get across the lesson that changed my teenage experience: True beauty is not about what you *see* on the outside but what you feel, sense and love from within.

Talina Sessler-Barker

Who Is Jack Canfield?

Jack Canfield is one of America's leading experts in the development of human potential and personal effectiveness. He is both a dynamic, entertaining speaker and a highly sought-after trainer. Jack has a wonderful ability to inform and inspire audiences toward increased levels of self-esteem and peak performance.

In addition to the *Chicken Soup for the Soul* series, Jack has coauthored numerous books, including his most recent release, *The Success Principles, How to Get From Where You Are to Where You Want to Be* with Janet Switzer, *The Aladdin Factor* with Mark Victor Hansen, *100 Ways to Build Self-Concept in the Classroom* with Harold C. Wells, *Heart at Work* with Jacqueline Miller and *The Power of Focus* with Les Hewitt and Mark Victor Hansen.

Jack is regularly seen on television shows such as Good Morning America, 20/20 and NBC Nightly News.

For further information about Jack's books, tapes and training programs, or to schedule him for a presentation, please contact:

Self-Esteem Seminars
P.O. Box 30880
Santa Barbara, CA 93130
Phone: 805-563-2935
Fax: 805-563-2945
Web: *www.chickensoupforthesoul.com*

Who Is Mark Victor Hansen?

In the area of human potential, no one is better known and more respected than Mark Victor Hansen. For more than thirty years, Mark has focused solely on helping people from all walks of life reshape their personal vision of what's possible.

He is a sought-after keynote speaker, bestselling author and marketing maven. Mark is a prolific writer with many best-selling books such as *The One Minute Millionaire, The Power of Focus, The Aladdin Factor* and *Dare to Win,* in addition to the *Chicken Soup for the Soul* series.

Mark has appeared on Oprah, CNN and The Today Show, and has been featured in *Time, U.S. News & World Report, USA Today, New York Times* and *Entrepreneur* and count-less radio and newspaper interviews.

As a passionate philanthropist and humani-tarian, he has been the recipient of numer-ous awards that honor his entrepreneurial spirit, philanthropic heart and business acu-men.

For further information on Mark's products and services, please contact:

Mark Victor Hansen & Associates, Inc.
P.O. Box 7665
Newport Beach, CA 92658
Phone: 949-764-2640
Fax: 949-722-6912
FREE resources online at:
www.markvictorhansen.com

Who Is Kimberly Kirberger?

Kimberly is the president and founder of Inspiration and Motivation for Teens, Inc. (I.A.M. for Teens, Inc.) a corporation formed entirely to work with and for teens and cofounder of the Teen Letter Project (T.L.P.), a group of teens responsible for answering the thousands of heartfelt letters received from teenagers. It is her strong belief that teens deserve recognition, a more positive image and better treatment within our society.

When she is not writing, Kimberly spends her time working for the empowerment of teenagers and the improvement of teen education. She has appeared as a teen consultant on television and radio shows, including Geraldo, MSNBC, Fox Family Channel's Parenting 101 and the Terry Bradshaw Show.

Kimberly is the author of the bestselling Teen Love series. She is coauthor of the *New York Times* bestseller, *Chicken Soup for the Teenage Soul;* the *New York Times* number-one bestseller *Chicken Soup for the Teenage Soul II; Chicken Soup for the Teenage Soul Journal* and

Chicken Soup for the College Soul. She is also coauthor of *Chicken Soup for the Parent's Soul.* Contact Kim at:

I.A.M. for Teens, Inc.
P.O. Box 936 • Pacific Palisades, CA 90272
phone: 310-573-3655 • fax: 310-573-3657
e-mail for stories and letters:
stories@teenagechickensoup.com
letters@teenagechickensoup.com
Web site: *www.teenagechickensoup.com*

Contributors

If you would like to contact any of the contributors for information about their writing or would like to invite them to speak in your community, look for their contact information included in their biography.

Sarah Barnett is a student and freelance writer in Ft. Worth, Texas. She has written many poems and other works for various publications including The National Library of Poetry and the Iliad Press. Her story was told to continually remind herself and others that such a simple thing, brought on by a simple person, can conquer so much. There are no limits. She can be reached via e-mail at *Duchess305@aol.com.*

Michele Bender is a freelance writer in New York City. She has written for many publications, including the *New York Times, Glamour, Jump, Cosmopolitan, Cosmo Girl, Ladies' Home Journal, Fitness* and *Marie Claire.* She can be reached via e-mail at *Mbender878@aol.com.*

Michelle Wallace Campanelli is a national

bestselling author. She was born on the Space Coast of Florida where she still resides with her husband, Louis. She is a graduate of Melbourne High School, Writers' Digest School and Keiser College. She is the author of *Hero of Her Heart,* by Blue Note Books and *Margarita,* by Hollis Books. She is also a short-story author in several nationally distributed anthologies published by Simon and Schuster's *Chocolate For a Woman's Heart* series. She has always enjoyed writing and painting as outlets for artistic expression. Currently, she is working on the sequel to *Margarita.* She can be reached via e-mail at *MCAMPANELLI@juno.com.*

Sydney Fox was born on November 1, 1982 in Tulsa, Oklahoma. Her parents' ministry to the homeless and the poor moved the family to the Washington, D.C. area. Helping the needy sparked her writing desires. It transformed daily journal entries into inspirational anecdotes about poverty's struggles. She works in a camera store and hopes to couple photography with her writings. She loves drama, plays the violin and cello and sings. She's planning her future and college major.

Lisa Rothbard is a seventeen-year-old senior in high school. She has been involved with the *Chicken Soup for the Teenage Soul* series since she was thirteen. She can be reached via e-mail at *Rothie99@hotmail.com.*

Talina Sessler-Barker, age twenty-three, graduated in 1998 from the University of Texas where she was a member of the Longhorn Cheerleading Squad. She currently teaches language arts and coaches cheerleading at Leander Middle School, while seeking her masters of education degree from Southwest Texas University. Her goal is to help young people realize that true beauty lies within themselves. She resides in Leander, Texas with her husband Donny.

Jane Denitz Smith is the author of two young adult novels, *Mary by Myself* (1994), and *Charlie Is a Chicken* (1998), both published by HarperCollins Publishers, and both Harper Trophy paperbacks. She is also the author of a board book, *Baby and Kitty and Mommy and Daddy* (Workman Publishing, 1994) and has written several plays, as well as novels. She writes and teaches in Williamstown, Massachusetts, where she lives with her husband and three children.

Elizabeth Stumbo will graduate as a member of the class of 2000. She participates in sports, scenery for school and community theaters, and is editor of her high-school yearbook. She hopes to pursue a career in the arts and communications field. She can be reached at P.O. Box 338, Ogden, IA 50212.

Julia Travis is a high-school junior in Livonia, Michigan, where she is class president and a member of the soccer team. Her work has been published in *A Celebration of Michigan's Young Poets—1999*. She would like to thank the friends who have always been there for her. She can be reached via e-mail at *Julesorama@aol.com.*

Cecile Wood is a British citizen, studying at the College of William and Mary in Virginia. She is currently doing a semester abroad in

Buenos Aires, Argentina. She is grateful to *Chicken Soup for the Soul* for giving her a chance to share her stories.

Supporting Teenagers

A portion of the profits that are generated from sales of the original edition of the bestseller, *Chicken Soup for the Teenage Soul III,* published in 2000 goes to various organizations that are doing important work for teens. Two of these organizations are:

Yellow Ribbon Project
Teen Letter Project

The Yellow Ribbon Project is a nonprofit organization that helps to prevent teen suicides.

Since its story first appeared in *A 3rd Serving of Chicken Soup for the Soul* and then again in *Chicken Soup for the Teenage Soul,* Yellow Ribbon has documented over 1,000 lives saved. We were deeply moved by Dale and Dar Emmes's dedication to preventing teen suicide because it came as a result of their losing their son to suicide. They have made hundreds of appearances at high schools and youth groups to discuss with teenagers this tragic epidemic and have marked results with each appearance.

To contact this organization for help in setting up a Yellow Ribbon Program in your school or community, or to receive a yellow ribbon for yourself and your friends:

Yellow Ribbon Project
P.O. Box 644 Westminster, CO 80030
phone: 303-426-4496
e-mail: light4life@yellowribbon.org
Web site: www.yellowribbon.org

The Teen Letter Project is responsible for answering the heartfelt letters received from teenagers and also reaching out to teens in trouble and encouraging them to seek professional help. The Project was founded by Kimberly Kirberger, along with Jack Canfield, Mark Victor Hansen and Health Communications, Inc. Contact:

Teen Letter Project
P.O. Box 936
Pacific Palisades, CA 90272
phone: 310-573-3655 fax: 510-573-3657
e-mail for stories and letters:
stories@teenagechickensoup.com
letters@teenagechickensoup.com
Web site: *www.teenagechickensoup.com*

More Chicken Soup?

We enjoy hearing your reactions to the stories in *Chicken Soup for the Soul* books. Please let us know what your favorite stories were and how they affected you.

Many of the stories and poems you enjoy in *Chicken Soup for the Soul* books are submitted by readers like you who had read earlier *Chicken Soup for the Soul* selections.

We invite you to contribute a story to one of these future volumes.

Stories may be up to 1,200 words and must uplift or inspire. To obtain a copy of our submission guidelines and a listing of upcoming *Chicken Soup* books, please write, fax or check our Web sites.

Chicken Soup for the Soul
P.O. Box 30880
Santa Barbara, CA 93130
fax: 805-563-2945
Web site: *www.chickensoup.com*

Also Available

Chicken Soup African American Soul
Chicken Soup Body and Soul
Chicken Soup Bride's Soul
Chicken Soup Caregiver's Soul
Chicken Soup Cat and Dog Lover's Soul
Chicken Soup Christian Family Soul
Chicken Soup Christian Soul
Chicken Soup College Soul
Chicken Soup Country Soul
Chicken Soup Couple's Soul
Chicken Soup Expectant Mother's Soul
Chicken Soup Father's Soul
Chicken Soup Fisherman's Soul
Chicken Soup Girlfriend's Soul
Chicken Soup Golden Soul
Chicken Soup Golfer's Soul, Vol. I, II
Chicken Soup Horse Lover's Soul
Chicken Soup Inspire a Woman's Soul
Chicken Soup Kid's Soul
Chicken Soup Mother's Soul, Vol. I, II
Chicken Soup Nature Lover's Soul
Chicken Soup Parent's Soul
Chicken Soup Pet Lover's Soul
Chicken Soup Preteen Soul, Vol. I, II
Chicken Soup Single's Soul
Chicken Soup Soul, Vol. I-VI
Chicken Soup at Work
Chicken Soup Sports Fan's Soul
Chicken Soup Teenage Soul, Vol. I-IV
Chicken Soup Woman's Soul, Vol. I, II
